Exile's Choice

Exile's Choice

Poems by

E. Martin Pedersen

© 2021 E. Martin Pedersen. All rights reserved.
This material may not be reproduced in any form, published,
reprinted, recorded, performed, broadcast,
rewritten or redistributed without
the explicit permission of E. Martin Pedersen.
All such actions are strictly prohibited by law.

Cover design by Shay Culligan

ISBN: 978-1-954353-20-6

Kelsay Books
502 South 1040 East, A-119
American Fork, Utah, 84003

Acknowledgments

Alexandria Quarterly: "Mood & Attitude."

Botticelli Magazine: "3 Gray Pleasures," "Yankee Go Home."

Cacti Fur: "As a Joke," "Time to Quit."

Dash: "Blind Man to Junkie."

Everest Magazine: "The Double Prayer."

Former People: "Gran Torino," "Gerrymandering the Great Unknown."

Frigg: "Camping with Charlie."

Muddy River Poetry Review: "The Great American West."

Mused: "Lay It On."

Peeking Cat Poetry: "Tourists."

Pilcrow & Dagger: "Orange Lifesavers."

Poetry Super Highway: "It's Not Late."

Strong Verse: "Yogaphobica."

Tower Journal: "Ashes."

Verse-Virtual: "[The writer writes a sad sad story]," "Gram," "Arms Across Breath," "Last Poem."

Several poems have been slightly revised.

Introduction

They say that the difference between exile and expatriation is the choice. When I came to Sicily in 1979 and stayed and stayed until today, that was my choice, right? Or did the island choose me? Between Scylla and Charybdis, the Sirens sing: run from/run to, familiar/strange, stay/leave, shoobie doobie. So, when living out of the red backpack lost its charm, I easily slid into a family-home-job so cozy that return became impractical, undesirable, near impossible. In a sense, I exiled myself. The choice I made made me.

"To go native"—is that the passage from ex-pat to exile? Am I denying my daily decision, imagining myself a victim of fate, the starry-eyed wanderer who can't find his way home? I don't know. The expression I hear most often from the locals here in Messina is: "Why don't you go back?" Back? Back in time, you mean? The San Francisco of my youth no longer exists. Neither do I as I left it.

"Oh. The people are so friendly! The food's so yummy! The architecture, the landscapes, the pretty girls and boys." No. That's tourist talk. Everyday life in Italy is full of dogshit. And spring flowers. And blank spaces. Like anywhere, everywhere.

Thus now, until the last boat leaves the isle, I write. My choice.

Contents

It's Not Late	13
Gran Torino	14
The Great American West	15
3 Gray Pleasures	17
Yankee Go Home	19
Orange Lifesavers	20
Tourists	22
[The writer writes a sad sad story]	23
Camping with Charlie	24
Gram	26
The Double Prayer	27
Ashes	28
Mood & Attitude	29
As a Joke	31
Blind Man to Junkie	32
Lay It On	33
Yogaphobica	34
Arms Across Breath	36
Gerrymandering the Great Unknown	37
Time to Quit	38
Last Poem	39

It's Not Late

It's not late but it seems
in the dark room with only
the blue glare of the silent screen
outside a rare car downstairs
they're not stomping around
in their wooden clogs
a hum, a welcome hum
window open, a fishing boat motor
on the glass mirror telling me
that the lights are still on
over in Italy.

Gran Torino

Gran Torino in the carport
Took Dad seven years to save up
He doesn't believe in buying on credit
He only buys American

Drove us to Yellowstone in that car
We camped beside the Utah road
I helped Dad set up the big tent
And cots for all us kids

Mom made mayonnaise and bologna sandwiches
With tomato slices, I wish I had one right now
On white bread with the crusts removed
And Tang, the astronaut's drink

We had it made back then, car games, singing
We were all still alive
Driving around Wyoming in the Gran Torino
Up ahead, a great life.

The Great American West

Flying over Utah
I see the creases
in my slacks
folds of sheets.

Nevada in the dark
reflex of the white line
pointing out of state
in either direction.

Golden hills a distance
tree tops out of range
the most handsome beaches
100 ft. down the cliffs
littered by the sea
spitting back stuff
caught in the teeth
of California.

Good shoes are needed
to take on Colorado
a clean state
with a nasty undertow
from the rocky coast
pushing cyclers uphill.

A dun horse would be happiest
a blue shirt would be happiest
red iron is happiest
a fried egg sandwich

and short bent trees growing tough
happiest in Wyoming.

And finally Arizona,
Mojave enough.

3 Gray Pleasures

I
The sad joy of a curb
the graded boundary, the sloped verge
a smooth gray concrete suburban curb
in California
after so long
so far away
a mighty swim
the trial and the prize
a glimpse
one last
clean
American
curb.

II
The strong librarian's lovely long gray hair
teach about the stars and how they pull
strict lessons with do-overs
it isn't real but, oh,
to live in that hair.

III
I dropped my key
to the bottom of the porta pot
reach down into the dung
years of build-up
past offenses and paper scraps
stiffening my arm
turning my head

holding my breath
pressing cautiously into the sinister unfamiliar
dense wet lifesource
to pluck out
a soft gray bone.

Yankee Go Home

I need to move to New Zealand
I hear it's paradise on Earth
the Kiwis I've met are the nicest
and the tattoos spectacular

Trent worked his ass off his whole life
mopping floors at the airport
taking shit from his supervisor
and his kids hated him

He quit and flew to New Zealand
got robbed on the way to the hostel
moved in with a family of sailors
until one drunk woman knifed him—
the damn Yankee.

Orange Lifesavers

A bear in a boat
No oars, no rudder, no sail
Polar bear in a dingy
Floating on choppy seas
    Did it eat the sailors?
    Is this life-raft from a sunken vessel?
    How did the bear get in the boat? Can it get out?
    Will it slowly starve or just bob around
    till it bumps into a beach?
Then go ashore
To re-join the rat-race.

I can see the bear from my space station in orbit—
Cutting edge tracking and zooming technology—
I watch it watching the water
Waiting for something to change
Yesterday it picked up an orange lifesaver
Smelt it, bit it, threw it back in the water,
We have plenty of experiments to do
Up here in the vacuum of outer space
Yet I focus on my vulnerable bear again
It's still there; it may even be there when I return to Earth
I know when I land, how many days are left
In my mission.

I still have photos of my family, but I have eaten all my candy
Waiting for answers to questions I can't be bothered to form
I think too much—a space disease

Music, poker, news, jokes don't interest me
Love would perhaps be nice, but that went the way of acne
I wouldn't have volunteered, in fact, in my youth
Now I may re-sign, I will
So I can observe how my white bear,
Lost in a blue ocean,
Gets out of trouble.

Tourists

Rustici mignon
Is that something you eat
      Are they these flour-coated thingees
They're cute
      I bet they're fried, watch out
This one's a rice ball
      With tomato sauce and ham and peas inside
In the center, how do they do that
      This one has white stuff, maybe melted cheese
Hope so
      Like a croissant or a pizza pocket
Shut up
      Rustics, if you ask me
Oh, there's an olive pit in this one, I almost busted a tooth
      Stuffed with bread crumbs within a fried bread crust
I don't like it
      Here's a tiny pizza extra small size, thick crust, of course
Like the people
      Not microwaved though, it's the real thing
Coke ... Pepsi
      Maybe they eat this for lunch
I like this one best with mushrooms
      I despise mushrooms, yuck
Here, give this a try
      What we going to wash it all down with
Yeah
      Yeah
Ask the boy what wine is recommended
With *rustici mignon.*

[The writer writes a sad sad story]

The writer writes a sad sad story
lost love; so sad the characters cry
and the writer enters the love story
and cries along with the sad characters,
then the man turns off the computer
he barely sees his reflection in the screen
eyes of despondency at lovesickness
wonder at the tears on his cheeks,
while his father lies gasping
in bed on the back side of the globe
the two tears could flood the land between
if the writer were able to walk on water
he would consider crossing the salt sea
to see his sad reflection one last time.

Camping with Charlie

I like to go camping with Charlie
There are maybe five or six people I can stand to go camping with
But Charlie's my favorite
He doesn't talk much during the day but he's just right
around the campfire
Never whines, that good cheer I'm envious of
We toss on our packs and we're off and up
The trail is clear and we don't need much rest
We like to get away from complications
Telephone holsters, mall music and sports bars
If he knows the name of a new flower he tells me.

In rivers and lakes we go skinny-dipping
When I see Charlie naked I think
He's just like me, handsome as hell
We meet people on the trail
I usually nod; Charlie often chats in his friendly way
He sets up camp while I cook dinner, we pack up our food
so the critters won't get it
After telling raunchy tales of glory, we wriggle
into our mummy bags
Lie on our backs and stare at the dark tent
Then we say g'night and sleep dead tired
It's okay, we both snore.

I have done enough and am ready to go
My nieces and nephews will be left with pleasant memories
So, I would gladly take Charlie's place lying there
Please let me take Charlie's place
Please.

If I can't take Charlie's place
At least let me lie next to him
Let me lie beside Charlie like we do when we go camping
Quiet in the dark, content like two cocoons
As I lie there I may feel jealous again
because Charlie gets to be born first
and fly off
in fields of green.

Gram

Took me into her walk-in closet
when I was only a boy
and for some reason
showed me her trophy
a funny bra with two lumps,
she explained that she'd had an operation long ago
cancer, which is bad
and had her breasts removed,
she'd been a nurse
so she knew the right words
I only sort of knew what she meant,
it was creepy to imagine
no female knockers
only scars and a fake bra.
Then we went into the kitchen
cloved ham and yams and berry pie
she'd made bread with homemade jam
the best I ever had in my life
one happy day at Gram's.

The Double Prayer

Carlos come in, I'm not well. I'll be alright but my hands are cold as ice. Come here, sit on the bed, it's okay, rub my hands. Harder, faster, closer, I'm so cold. I'll be alright, but I may need to go out when your father gets home.

    Better? Not much really. Don't stop, Carlos, my fingers are still so cold. I don't know why. You don't usually see me without makeup, huh? When you father comes we'll go for a doctor. You stay here and get your own supper. Don't worry, everything's fine. We'll call as soon as we know something. Thanks for rubbing my hands, that helped a lot.

Ashes

Cremains, they're called now
I didn't know that term
I didn't know it would cost so much
To make Papa burn.

Counting out hundred dollar bills
Trying correctly to mourn
Then looking at old photographs
Of when Papa was born.

Born to burn
A daring adventure

He smiled more in his youth
He got so tired, he just gave up
To tell the truth.

And we will have a service
To respect his memory
There might be crying
Then his ashes will blow away
Into the indifferent sea.

Mood & Attitude

When I found out I was dying
I started going to the park
every day to watch the ducks
mothers and children swings
breathe grass gardeners broken lights
patting the bench
the empty stage
I'd sit alone an audience
of one for the silent
mystery play, the miracle
play beside the slide
boys and girls watching each
other scared to pump
higher. I don't talk to them
but I like to watch this
world spin around me
with a half-smile, I
look up the mothers' legs
up up at the oak galls at
lovers on a blanket reeking of hormones
the mirror at the center of the merry
go round watching the horses
alive winnowing
prance the cakewalk
kick back their heads
and laugh out loud.

I am the terminal reflection
the sundial on the ground shadowing a cold bronze circle
—tick tock is telling me to ghost it.

I know exactly what the red
fish under the miniature bridge
are thinking
and what the black fish
are thinking, the mind games
they play,
but if I ignore them they cease
to exist
just like myself
in this city park.

As a Joke

As a joke, you went to get your mocha

then sat at a nearby table ignoring me

it worked; I fell in love with you again watching

yet I got jealous of others looking at you too

then grew tired of the game

on the way home we fought

about whose turn it was to choose a TV show

I went to bed mad and slept like a cat

constantly opening my eyes to check.

Blind Man to Junkie

That guy I was talking to
just took my radio
no back, no batteries
the one I carried all day
pretending music
as I walked around the same block
in downtown San Jose.
Don't worry honey
I'll defend you
I'll get it back
I know that guy.
You mean he's a junkie
like you, Jean?
Let me help you cross the street
I don't want to cross the street
What do you want?
I want my radio.

Lay It On

Loading my shotgun for personal safety
Carrying it to show my boss at work
Where we all face cutbacks and lay-offs
I'm the only one who defied the jerk.

They abused me but I said 'no'
There is a limit you have crossed
Now you threaten and slander and shove
I'm going to have a little chat with my boss.

I think our meeting went well considering
It felt good to clear the air
I showed the boss it was nothing personal,
When I laid it all out on the table
All he did was stare.

Yogaphobica

A man climbs into the upper part of the wardrobe surprised
it will still hold his weight and closes the doors
pulling out his fingers just in time
curls into a ball sideways
knees to chest
feet tucked in and head bowed
hands pressed to ears in the dark
if it ever passes.

Standing straight up
stretched
stiff as an ironing board
against the door jam
chest puffs, whispers
you do not need
to show
that you are a man,
you glorious
lightning bolt nuclear core telephone pole to Hell,
on the very spot that makes the human body
the axis of the earth and solar system
at the very least.

Lying comfortably
inside a slow flow mountain stream
cool gray stones deep green moss sierra pure shadows
of trees dropping exquisitely occasional leaves
looking up at the baby blue sky and play-party clouds
shimmering saran blanket of calm abiding
see myself

under the glassy reflection from above
my hands hold my chest down
I rest
wet and refreshed, whole and caressed,
headed downstream.

These are the exercises we all do.
This is the discipline of measurement.

Arms Across Breath

In a chair of whispers
by a house made of living wood
a mile above the crystal beach
I can't smell the salt
but the waterfalls cough and spit
blue birds jaw
butterflies snap their wings
a pine tree stretches
with a moan and a crackle
the grass eye the flowers with envy
as the sun arrives expectedly

All the sleeping grandchildren on earth and underground
breathe across easy deserts and mountains
blessing my forearms.

Gerrymandering the Great Unknown

You need an edge, a profit margin
that one good idea, a winner
say "I don't want to die"
when all the packaging, the styrofoam peanuts
gone, all the peanuts gone
you stand at the edge of the black hole of gravity
feet first or head first
cry "I don't want to go"
then go.

You can't touch this imaginary boundary
but you can see it from here
all the tricks you ever knew are worthless
the mystery chord, the 'love yous'
an empty echo of the quantum self
ratcheting up
to the great unknown.

Time to Quit

I do love my chips and beer
But it's time to quit
I've had bushels and barrels
And been content
But my doc agrees
It's time to quit

A life of work
A handful of pebbles
My garden needs attention
I only wanted to help
Not sure I did my duty
I'm tired now

Can't go on forever
Time to quit and yet
My dear, I love you lots
I won't quit you
I will never quit you
I'll hang on to keep from drowning
Or dying of thirst.

Last Poem

Last words—
In heaven there is
No beer
No language
No facial expression
No need
You get one chance
To fail
To express
In a code
Secret to ourselves
Then the bear
Eats your soul
The crow
Your eyes
The worms
Your tongue.

About the Author

E. Martin Pedersen, originally from San Francisco, has lived for 40 years in eastern Sicily, where he teaches English at the local university. His poetry has appeared most recently in Ginosko Literary Journal, Abstract Magazine, Neologism Poetry Journal, Poesis, Thirteen Myna Birds. Martin is an alumnus of the Squaw Valley Community of Writers. His collection of haiku, *Bitter Pills,* came out in June 2020.

www.ingramcontent.com/pod-product-compliance
Lightning Source LLC
Chambersburg PA
CBHW021029090426
42738CB00007B/946